ANIMAL MASTERMINDS

Nookie's Daring Rescue!

Supersmart Dog

BY SARAH EASON
ILLUSTRATED BY LUDOVIC SALLÉ

BEARPORT
PUBLISHING

Minneapolis, Minnesota

Credits: 20, © Belovodchenko Anton/Shutterstock; 21, © Konstantin Zaykov/Shutterstock; 22, © SasaStock/Shutterstock; 23, © Yakobchuk Viacheslav/Shutterstock.

Bearport Publishing Company Product Development Team
President: Jen Jenson; Director of Product Development: Spencer Brinker; Senior Editor: Allison Juda; Editor: Charly Haley; Associate Editor: Naomi Reich; Senior Designer: Colin O'Dea; Associate Designer: Elena Klinkner; Associate Designer: Kayla Eggert; Product Development Assistant: Anita Stasson

Produced by Calcium
Editor: Jennifer Sanderson; Proofreader: Harriet McGregor; Designer: Paul Myerscough; Picture Researcher: Rachel Blount

DISCLAIMER: This graphic story is a dramatization based on true events. It is intended to give the reader a sense of the narrative rather than a presentation of actual details as they occurred.

Library of Congress Cataloging-in-Publication Data

Names: Eason, Sarah, author. | Salle, Ludovic, 1985- illustrator.
Title: Nookie's daring rescue! : supersmart dog / by Sarah Eason ; illustrated by Ludovic Salle.
Description: Minneapolis, Minnesota : Bearport Publishing, [2023] | Series: Animal masterminds | Includes bibliographical references and index.
Identifiers: LCCN 2022036035 (print) | LCCN 2022036036 (ebook) | ISBN 9798885094337 (hardcover) | ISBN 9798885095556 (paperback) | ISBN 9798885096706 (ebook)
Subjects: LCSH: Rescue dogs--Anecdotes--Juvenile literature. | Rescue dogs--Anecdotes--Comic books, strips, etc.
Classification: LCC SF428.55 .E27 2023 (print) | LCC SF428.55 (ebook) | DDC 636.7/0886--dc23/eng/20220822
LC record available at https://lccn.loc.gov/2022036035
LC ebook record available at https://lccn.loc.gov/2022036036

For more information, write to Bearport Publishing, 5357 Penn Avenue South, Minneapolis, MN 55419.

Contents

CHAPTER 1

The Hiking Husky

Girdwood, Anchorage, Alaska. Scott Swift was looking for a dog to adopt.

THIS IS NANOOK. WE CALL HIM NOOKIE FOR SHORT.

HEY, FELLA! DO YOU WANT TO BE MY TRAIL BUDDY?

HE'D BE GREAT OUTDOORS. HE'S AN ALASKAN HUSKY.

THAT'S A SMART **BREED**, RIGHT?

YES, AND THEY ARE VERY INDEPENDENT!

I THINK THAT'S A GREAT SIGN OF INTELLIGENCE.

I AGREE. THEY'RE TERRIFIC AT TAKING CARE OF THEMSELVES AND **NAVIGATING**.

GREAT! I'LL TAKE HIM.

Over the next few years, Scott and Nookie had many adventures together.

Nookie also went on solo adventures along the nearby Crow Pass Trail. Sometimes, he joined hikers on this 25-mile* path through the wilderness. But he was always home in time for bed.

*40-km

Then, when Nookie was about seven years old, he didn't return for a few days. Scott was worried until he got a phone call.

HEY, SCOTT, ITS AHNAH. NOOKIE WAS FOUND ON THE CROW PASS TRAIL. CAN YOU COME PICK HIM UP?

THANK GOODNESS YOU FOUND HIM. I HAVE BEEN SO WORRIED. HE'S BEEN GONE FOR THREE NIGHTS.

NOOKIE MADE SOME FRIENDS ON THE TRAIL AND BROUGHT THEM TO THE NATURE CENTER.

THAT'S A 4 HOUR DRIVE ROUNDTRIP!

Scott was called several times over the summer.

COME FETCH NOOKIE, SCOTT!

NOOKIE'S HERE AGAIN!

THAT DOG OF YOURS DROPPED BY!

I'M SO SORRY IF HE GAVE YOU TROUBLE.

ARE YOU KIDDING? HE'S SO FRIENDLY AND HELPFUL. THAT'S ONE SMART DOG! WE'D STILL BE LOST IF IT HADN'T BEEN FOR NOOKIE.

Scott was proud of Nookie and made a new tag for his collar.

NOOKIE
CROW PASS GUIDE DOG
Return to
Scott Swift

CHAPTER 2
Trail Disaster

Later that summer, Amelia Milling was saying goodbye to her friend Billie. She was heading to the Crow Pass Trail.

On the second day of her hike, the 21-year-old slipped on some snow. Amelia slid more than 300 feet* down the slope into a boulder.

*Amelia is deaf and communicates using American Sign Language.

*91 m

Suddenly, Nookie appeared!

Nookie helped Amelia get up and find her way back to the trail. Her leg was badly hurt, but she could still walk.

The next morning...

YOU'RE STILL HERE! ARE YOU READY TO GET GOING, BOY?

The pair followed the trail until they came to Eagle River. To cross, they had to go through freezing, fast-moving water.

Suddenly, Amelia fell in.

ARGH!

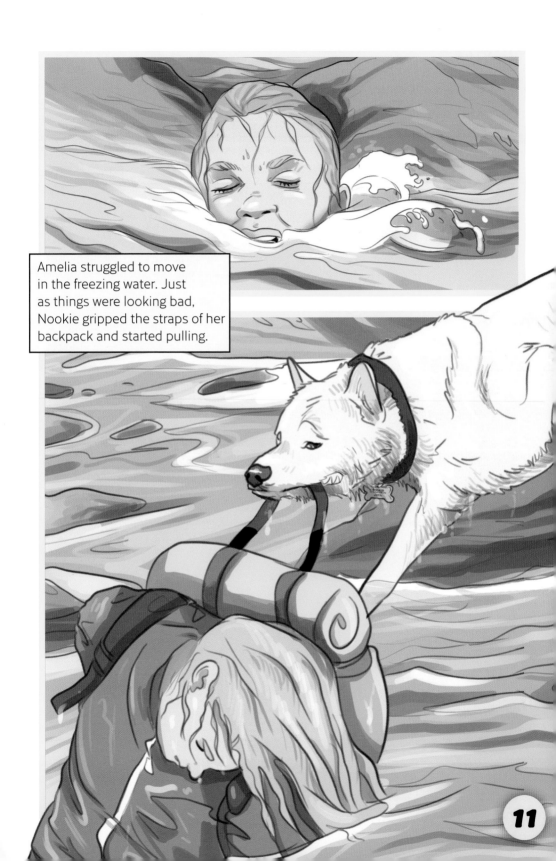

Amelia struggled to move in the freezing water. Just as things were looking bad, Nookie gripped the straps of her backpack and started pulling.

CHAPTER 3

Rescued!

After reaching the bank, Amelia felt dazed. She knew **hypothermia** could set in quickly. It was time to press her special **SOS** device.

BUZZ!

DON'T WORRY, BOY. HELP WILL BE HERE SOON.

Amelia took out her sleeping bag and got inside to keep warm.

Nookie stayed with Amelia on the side of the river for several hours. Whenever Amelia started to fall asleep, Nookie licked her face to try to keep her awake.

Eventually, Alaskan state troopers in a helicopter found Amelia with Nookie beside her.

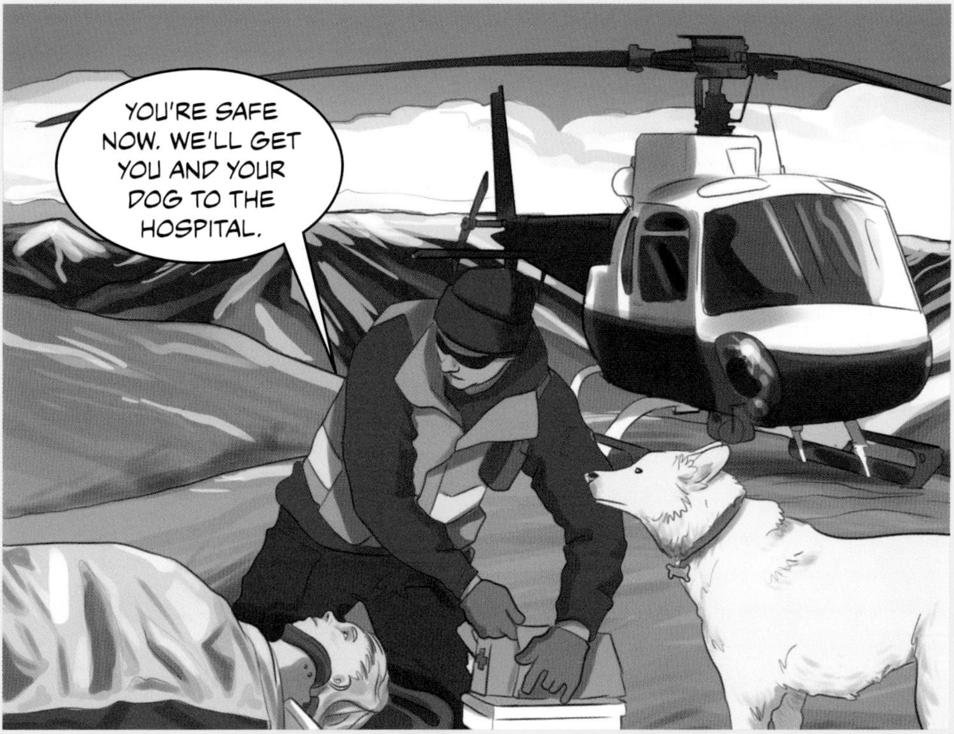
YOU'RE SAFE NOW. WE'LL GET YOU AND YOUR DOG TO THE HOSPITAL.

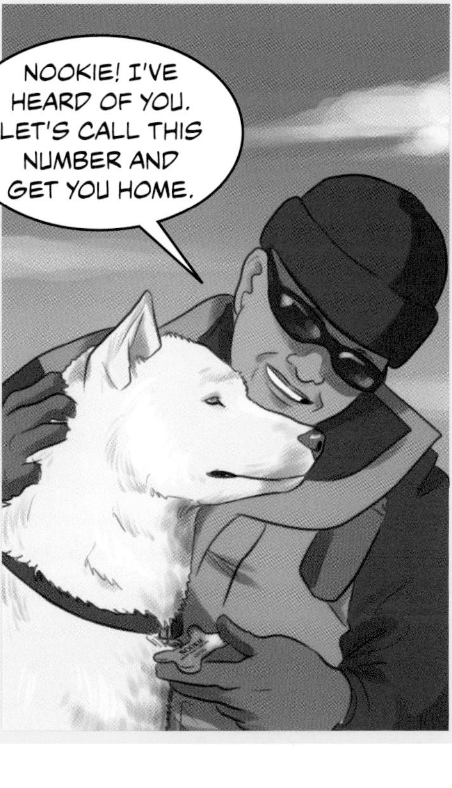
NOOKIE! I'VE HEARD OF YOU. LET'S CALL THIS NUMBER AND GET YOU HOME.

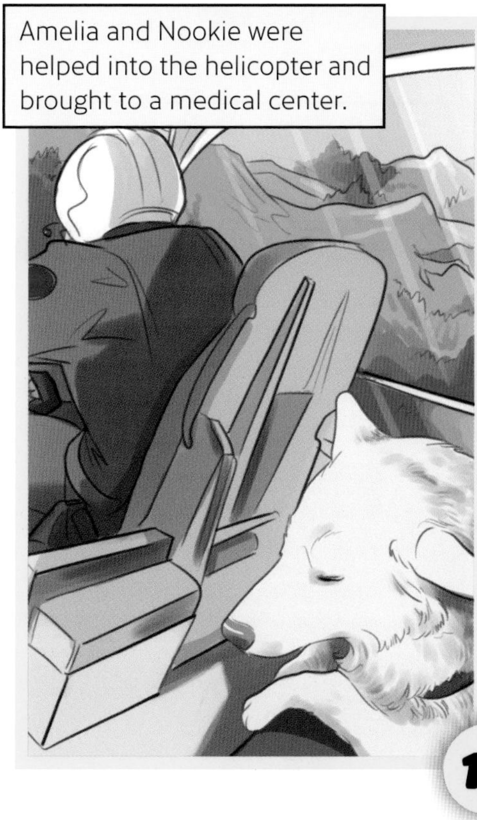
Amelia and Nookie were helped into the helicopter and brought to a medical center.

CHAPTER 4
Lifesaver

After Amelia was safely at the hospital, a trooper delivered Nookie back to Scott.

NOOKIE IS ONE SMART DOG, SCOTT! HE HAS AMAZING **ADAPTIVE INTELLIGENCE**.

WHAT'S THAT?

IT'S HIS ABILITY TO LEARN AND THINK INDEPENDENTLY— TO SOLVE PROBLEMS. THAT DOG IS SO SMART HE COULD BE FAMOUS!

That gave Scott an idea. He started a Facebook page for people to share pictures and stories of Nookie.

I CAN'T BELIEVE ALL THESE PEOPLE ARE POSTING STORIES ABOUT YOU, NOOKIE!

YOU'VE BEEN ON HIKES WITH SO MANY PEOPLE!

LINDSEY HONEMANN SAYS SHE WAS HIKING THE CROW PASS TRAIL WITH HER FRIENDS. YOU JOINED ALONG, AS THOUGH YOU WERE GUIDING THEM.

WHEN SHE PASSED A WATERFALL, SHE SLIPPED ON AN ICY ROCK. LINDSEY FELL AND STARTED TO SLIDE TOWARD A CLIFF.

SHE SAYS IF YOU HADN'T BEEN THERE TO GRAB HER THAT DAY, SHE WOULDN'T HAVE SURVIVED.

17

A few months later, there was a knock at Scott's door. It was Amelia and Billie.

WHAT A SURPRISE!

HAVE YOU HEARD THE NEWS? NOOKIE IS NOW AN HONORARY ALASKA STATE TROOPER...

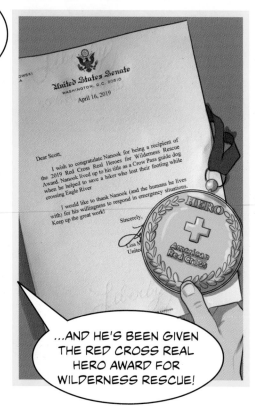

...AND HE'S BEEN GIVEN THE RED CROSS REAL HERO AWARD FOR WILDERNESS RESCUE!

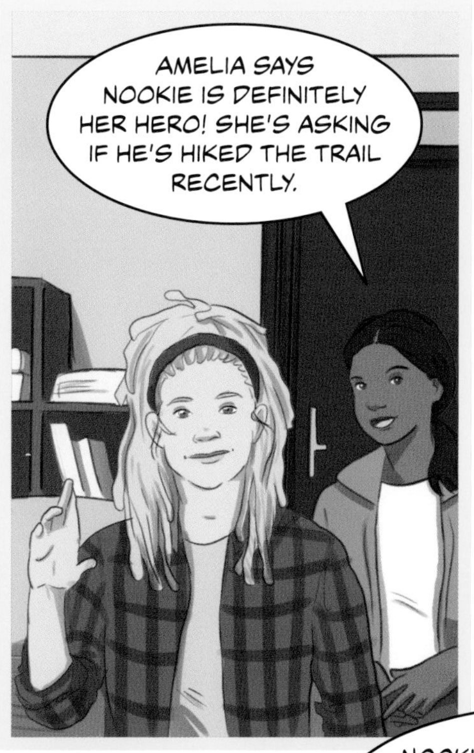
AMELIA SAYS NOOKIE IS DEFINITELY HER HERO! SHE'S ASKING IF HE'S HIKED THE TRAIL RECENTLY.

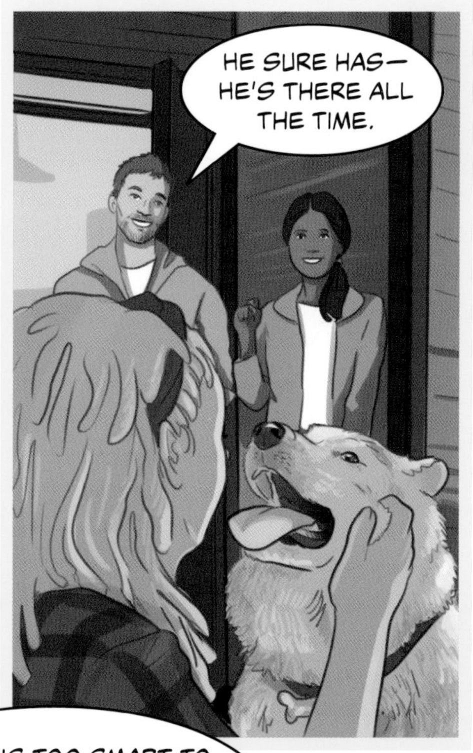
HE SURE HAS—HE'S THERE ALL THE TIME.

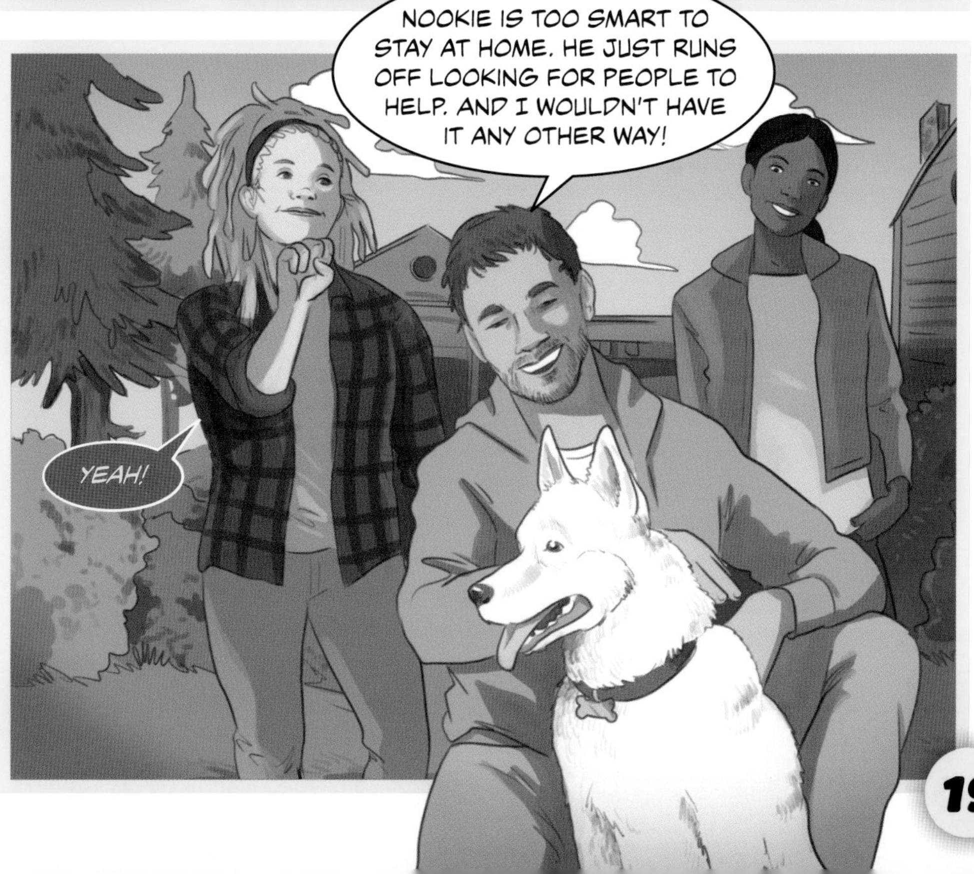
NOOKIE IS TOO SMART TO STAY AT HOME. HE JUST RUNS OFF LOOKING FOR PEOPLE TO HELP. AND I WOULDN'T HAVE IT ANY OTHER WAY!
YEAH!

All about Huskies

Huskies are tough dogs that can live in very cold places. They have a thick coat of fur to keep them warm. There are many types of huskies. The Alaskan husky is one of them. Let's learn more facts about these supersmart animals!

- Alaskan huskies can grow as tall as 25 inches (65 cm) and weigh up to 75 pounds (30 kg).

- Alaskan huskies were first used as working dogs. People used these dogs to pull sleds through the snow. Today, they are often used in sled dog racing competitions.

- Known for their ability to run quickly and for long distances, Alaskan huskies are very athletic. They can run 28 miles per hour (45 kph) and travel almost 1,000 miles (1,600 km) in a little over 8 days!

TODAY, HUSKIES ARE MAINLY USED AS SLED DOGS FOR SPORT OR FUN.

SIBERIAN HUSKIES ARE KNOWN FOR THEIR BLUE EYES.

- Alaskan huskies are closely **related** to two other types of huskies. These are Alaskan malamutes and Siberian huskies.

- Alaskan malamutes were around 2,000 to 3,000 years ago. These dogs get their name from the people who first worked with the dogs, the Mahlemut.

- In the late 1800s, Siberian huskies were brought to Alaska from **Siberia**, in Russia. Like Alaskan huskies, they were used as working dogs to pull sleds through the snow.

More Smart Dogs

In South Carolina, a supersmart border collie named Chaser was taught to recognize words. Her owner, Dr. John Pilley, taught her colors. Then, he put a blue ball in front of her and told her to find blue. Chaser picked up the ball and brought it to her owner. Next, John put the ball in another room and Chaser found the blue ball. By the end of her life, Chaser had learned more than 1,000 words!

COLLIES ARE VERY INTELLIGENT DOGS.

One day, marine Terry McGlade collapsed while he was walking his dog, Major. The Labrador retriever-pit bull mix jumped into action. Major had been trained to help when Terry had **seizures**. The dog pulled Terry's phone from his pocket and called 911. Major saved Terry's life.

Glossary

adaptive intelligence the ability to learn from your surroundings and solve problems with that knowledge

breed a type of animal that looks and acts a certain way

hypothermia a condition in which a person's body temperature becomes dangerously low

navigating finding where someone needs to go from where they are

related belonging to the same family or group

seizures sudden attacks that can cause a person to shake and lose consciousness

Siberia a very cold part of northern Russia

SOS an international sign of distress that is used when someone is in need of help

SOME DOGS USE THEIR ADAPTIVE INTELLIGENCE TO DO IMPORTANT JOBS.

Index

Read More

Jaycox, Jaclyn. *Read All about Dogs (Read All about It).*
North Mankato, MN: Capstone Press, 2021.

Mattern, Joanne. *Dogs (The World's Smartest Animals).*
Minneapolis: Bellwether Media, 2021.

Oachs, Emily Rose. *Sporting Dogs (Dog Groups).*
Minneapolis: Bellwether Media, 2021.

Learn More Online

1. Go to **www.factsurfer.com** or scan the QR code below.
2. Enter "**Nookie's Daring Rescue**" into the search box.
3. Click on the cover of this book to see a list of websites.